TRINITY GUILDHALL

Piano Grade 1

Pieces & Exercises
for Trinity Guildhall examinations

2012-2014

Published by
Trinity College London

Registered Office:
89 Albert Embankment
London SE1 7TP UK

T +44 (0)20 7820 6100
F +44 (0)20 7820 6161
E music@trinityguildhall.co.uk
www.trinityguildhall.co.uk

Registered in the UK
Company no. 02683033
Charity no. 1014792

Copyright © 2011 Trinity College London

Unauthorised photocopying is illegal
No part of this publication may be copied or reproduced in any
form or by any means without the prior permission of the publisher.

Printed in England by Halstan & Co. Ltd, Amersham, Bucks.

Gigue in G

Georg Philipp Telemann
(1681-1767)

Dynamics and articulation are editorial.

Menuett in F

from *Notebook for Nannerl*

collected by Leopold Mozart
(1719-1787)

Allegro in G

Carl Czerny
(1791-1857)

Allegretto

Franz Wohlfahrt
(1833–1884)

Our Old Stove is Bust Again

Traditional *arr.* Petr Eben
(1929-2007)

Saturday Stomp

Carol Barratt

The Very Vicious Velociraptor

Pauline Hall and Paul Drayton

Cat's Whiskers

Elissa Milne

Walking Together

Christopher Norton

Moderato [♩. = 54–63]

*Composer's metronome mark ♩. = c. **60**.*

Copyright © 1990 by Boosey & Hawkes Music Publishers Ltd.
Reproduced by permission of Boosey & Hawkes Music Publishers Ltd.

Exercises

1a. Toast and Jam – tone, balance and voicing

1b. Two at a Time – tone, balance and voicing

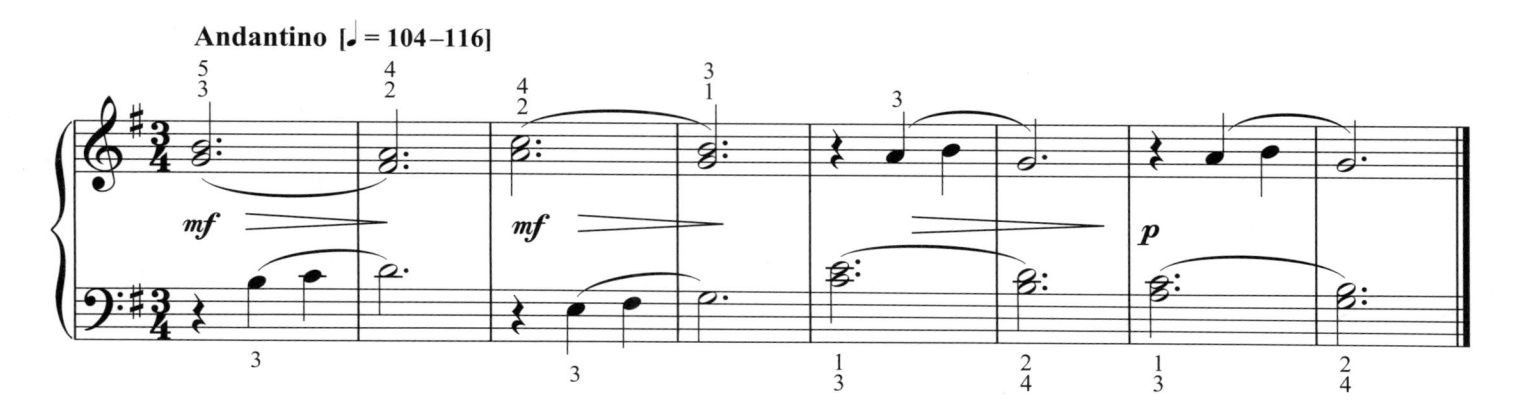

2a. Hill and Dale – co-ordination

Copyright © 2011 Trinity College London

2b. Scherzo – co-ordination

Lively and playfully [♩ = 126–144]

3a. Up and Under – finger & wrist strength and flexibility

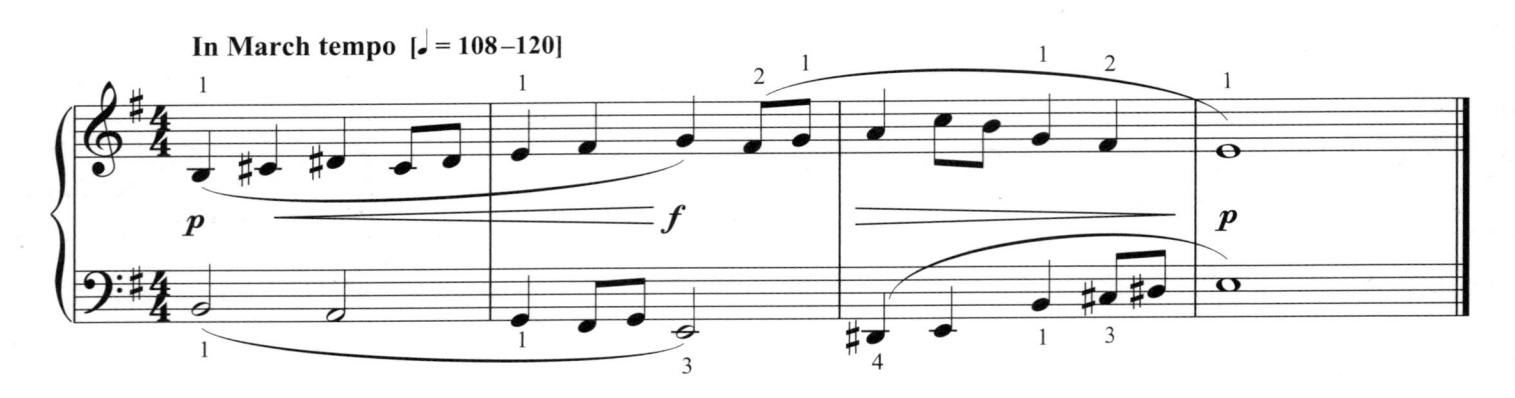

In March tempo [♩ = 108–120]

3b. Moving Out, Moving In – finger & wrist strength and flexibility

Lento [♩. = 52–60]